I0141704

"NEVER, NEVER GIVE UP"

by

B. GALE CHANCE

Published by:
Creative Press
P.O. Box 769000
Dallas, TX 75224

Copyright © 2014

ISBN#978-0-89985-483-0

All rights reserved under International Copyright Law.
Written permission must be secured from the publisher to
reproduce, copy, or transmit any part of this book.

Cover Design: Brandon Groomer

TABLE OF CONTENTS

INTRODUCTION

Serenity Prayer
God grant me the serenity to accept the things I cannot change, courage to change the things I can and wisdom to know the difference.

My thoughts have been, "What can I change, what must I accept and how can I make my situation better?" I have learned many lessons about patience and endurance. In six decades my motto has been, "Never, never give up." But even if I knew God was with me, I took matters into my own hands. I took courses of near destruction and veered off the path He had planned. My question was often, "Why? Why me? Why now? Just why?"

It shouldn't have taken most of my life to surrender all and receive the joy and peace that was mine all along. I encourage you to seek and accept your own joy and peace God has created for you without going through what I have experienced.

Chapter 1

MY BEGINNING

My family is from what started out as small textile mill villages along the Chattahoochee River in west Georgia, east Alabama. About 50 years ago these villages were totally mill owned houses, a general store and medical provisions. The river not only was a geographic divide, but a cultural one as well.

The Georgia side of the river was where the mill owners, managers and 'other than' mill employees usually lived. The mill labor force for the most part lived in five villages that covered about a 15 mile stretch of the river. The mills were located on the river, but the railroad was an easy way to bring raw products to the mills and to take the finished product from the mills. The houses in the villages were constructed by the mills and then sold to the workers. The houses were almost duplicates of all the other houses.

Over the years, families might add a room or a porch to alternate the appearance, but mostly they were all just mill houses. Workers could purchase groceries from the general store and have the totals taken from their weekly salary. Often, the pay outs went right back to the mill to pay for the families' living expenses, in a vicious cycle of never getting ahead.

The raw farm cotton was delivered to each mill by rail, truck, or horse-wagon, where the process would start in the carding room using machines to mix and clean the field cotton. The cotton was then spun into thread; large spools of thread would be delivered to the spinning room where the weaving process took place.

I'm sure the mill work was not nearly as hard as I might remember, but the work was repetitious, long hours, dirty and without possibility of promotion. The weave room looked cloudy on most days because of the lint in the air. The cotton lint filled your nostrils. As the looms blared so loudly, sign language was the only method of communication.

Most of my entire family at one time or another has worked in the weave room of one of the mills. The workers who could hold out for fifty years were given a potluck dinner and gold watch as they retired to live on what small social security benefits they had earned. My mother was allowed to begin working at the age of fourteen and remained there, with short child-bearing leaves, for 48 years. Her lack of dedication to the mill didn't warrant another two years to earn the dinner and watch. Although my mother could read the weekly newspaper, her Bible and do her numbers, her education was extremely limited.

I was born after six months of gestation, weighing less

than three pounds. Mother had already lost two infants. In the mid forties, and in our rural area, premature infants had little hope of survival. My sister was twelve, a brother was two, and a half brother was eighteen. My half brother told me I was so small he put me in his shirt pocket and left the hospital, never paying for me. He would kid me later that they might come get me someday to take me back for non-payment. I was told the doctors informed my family I would survive only if I was a born fighter. I was taken to the small frame house, put in a wooden box on the coal burning stove door for warmth. I guess I was a born fighter and became, for the most part, a healthy child.

Our family was very private, not discussing issues but letting them be the "elephant" in the corner. They were there; they just weren't discussed or resolved. My father left home when I was three, but I was in my teens before I fully understood that he had 'run off' with his niece to Atlanta where they established a life together as a common law couple. I was told my father was a member of the Ku Klux Klan (KKK), who had in fact been kicked out of the clan and had a cross burned in our front yard because of his affairs, many with women of color. My sister had left home when I was five, leaving just my mother, brother and me as a family unit.

My father was gone for about seven years before I remember his return. His sister, my Aunt Susie Mae, still lived in town where he would stay when he came for visits, but only four to five times a year. My father never came to get my brother and me from my mother's house, but a phone call would be received and we would wait for the taxi to come.

My brother and I would go to Aunt Susie Mae's on Saturday morning, spend the night and be sent back home Sunday afternoon. My father would spend most of his visit drinking beer and playing poker with adult cousins, as my brother and I spent the days playing with our cousins in the yard.

On Sundays, Aunt Susie Mae would cook large country dinners; these might include fried chicken, mashed potatoes, fried okra, corn bread, and banana pudding for dessert. The men would be called to the table to eat, the women would eat, and then, the children would be called last. Often, by the time the children were called, most of the country dinner was gone, and we would be served pineapple sandwiches. I still hate pineapple sandwiches.

In our community, divorce was uncommon and I remember no other child in my grade not having a father at home. Most of my schoolmates' fathers worked in the mill, while their mother's stayed home as housewives. The housewives would do their best to grow and can many of the family vegetables.

They often had chickens peeking in the backyard. The chickens would provide the eggs and later the meat for their families. We lived there during the times where each small community had a milkman who would deliver bottles of fresh milk to the doorsteps. Since my mother would be at work on milk delivery days, the milkman would go into our house by the unlocked front door and leave the milk in our refrigerator.

My mother, being the only wage earner, usually worked six days a week, which left my brother and I alone much of the time. Because Mother would have to be at the mill early, my brother and I started at an early age in getting ourselves up, feeding ourselves, dressing, and then going off to school on our own.

I even remember my first day of school. Mother was at work, I was told by my brother which classroom I was to go in. The other children were brought to school by their mothers, and their first day of school was a celebration. I remember sitting in the back of the room waiting to be told what to do.

About mid-morning, the teacher, Miss Wheeler, called me to the front and asked me who I was and where my mother was. I told her Mother was at work and my brother had told me to come in and take a seat. Miss Wheeler had been my brother's teacher and before she asked the question, I believed she already knew our Mother was at work.

That was perhaps the beginning of my dislike for school. Because my mother was usually at work, she wasn't involved in my class parties, PTO (Parent Teacher Organization) or class performances. And when my school work began to be difficult, I was told to do the best I could. I made poor grades and developed a learning disability, mostly in reading, spelling and phonetics.

Chapter 2

AN ANGELIC VISITATION

When my father began coming around, a huge "elephant" appeared, and at the age of ten, his incest began. Toward evening when he was in town, I would be called into the bedroom, where he would spend time teaching me how to "be a woman," as he called it. The lights were always left off in the bedroom when my father and I were there, which added a sense of fear. I can't even remember my father's voice, as he seldom spoke to me.

From a church pastor, I remembered a message he had told to young people who couldn't sleep at night, mostly from the fear of the unknown. He suggested that the kids hold their hands up toward the ceiling like they were reaching for God. But I knew my "unknown," and couldn't raise my hands. At those times, I would say my own prayers asking someone to save me.

But things never got better; it went on for years. From time-to-time we might go fishing, but we never caught any fish. Or we might go alone for a drive in the country. My brother always thought I was loved more than he was because our father would not take him with us on these special outings.

For about six years, the abuse continued. I didn't know what to call it; I just knew it wasn't right. I prayed each night when we were at Aunt Susie Mae's that I could go to sleep before he called me back, or when he wanted to go for a ride that my brother could go with us. My father had always said I had to keep our special times secret because other people wouldn't understand the special relationship we had. They would think I was a bad girl, and I would be sent away; my mother would not be allowed to keep me. I believed everyone in my life knew what was happening but chose not to disturb the "elephant."

About the same time the abuse began, I started having seizures and migraine headaches. I would lose consciousness for perhaps only seconds, but fall to the floor and for twenty to thirty minutes I felt disoriented, unable to focus enough to know where I was. After several seizures, my mother decided to take me to the doctor to get medicine. I was diagnosed with what the doctor just called petit mal seizures.

They occurred at home, stores, churches, family member houses and schools. Mother would do her best to get me up and out as quickly as possible to avoid being noticed. This "elephant" was also kept as secret as possible. I suffered my first seizure on Christmas Day. And when we arrived to see our father, I was treated like a princess. The only gift I ever remember receiving from him, I received that year—a princess doll. It was a beautiful doll with long white dress and black patent leather shoes. I was allowed to sit on Aunt Susie Mae's bed in the front room all day. A Christmas to remember!

Over the years I knew my mother loved me, she just didn't express it in ways that I felt were encouraging. I remember when I was ten years old and I had a chest cold. She had made a mustard plaster for my chest; it had been heated too much and it burned my skin when it was applied. Through my sobs, I heard her say she was sorry and for the first time in my life, I heard her say, "I love you." I was an adult before I remember hearing her say those words again.

At the age of twelve, I was visiting my sister at her home in another state during the summer break. Her home was in a development with new houses being built beside and in back of her house. One evening as dew was falling, I was asked to take the dogs to the back yard and put them in the pen for the night. My brother-in-law used the dogs for rabbit hunting and they weren't left to run around the yard at night.

Workers from the house behind their house had gone home for the day but had left their power cord plugged into the power source of the house next door. I remember reaching for the power cord that was lying over the top of the pen, and then I could feel myself being whipped around on the ground by the surge of electricity that was going through my body; I was being electrocuted.

The next moment, I was above the ground—watching. I saw my brother-in-law run to the house next door to pull the cord out of the outlet; I saw my sister running around to the back of the house; I could hear the neighbors shouting out, "What's wrong," and I heard the cries of my niece and nephew.

I remember a person being with me as I watched the scene. It was getting dark, but around me there seemed to be a light source; we were standing in a beautiful place. I could even see over the treetops, but I wasn't afraid of what was happening. When I realized an angel was there beside me, my first thought was that I had died, and she had come to take me to Heaven. I could see a tunnel ahead of us filled with brilliant white fog that even sparkled.

I was so overwhelmed I don't remember talking; I was just trying to make sense of what was happening and thinking, "I must be dreaming." I know there was music playing, but I didn't concentrate on it long enough to remember what was played at my first death. When the beautiful angel finally spoke, she said, "You can't come now, you have to go back. You're not ready."

The next moment, I was being helped to my feet by my family. I had no burns and no noticeable injury. I often wondered what the person, who had been above the trees with me, meant. "That I wasn't ready?" I was checked out by a doctor who also reported, "No noticeable injury."

Although this happened before lawsuits were the way to settle wrongs, the construction company sent an attorney to our humble home to express the company's apology for any trauma I may have suffered. Mother explained I was fine and needed no money. The attorney was quick to ask my mother to sign a waiver to dismiss any future action and gladly gave her twenty-five dollars to sign the form. I often wondered what kind of bonus the attorney received for getting a settlement so cheaply. This incident began my lifelong joy of having my personal angel to watch over me.

Chapter 3

POPULARITY HAS ADVANTAGES

One of the strongest, most powerful lessons I learned from my mother was about faith. The mill workers were paid in cash each Thursday for the previous week's work. Remember that in the fifties and sixties women were paid a great deal less than men, and our father didn't pay child support.

When my mother came home with her week's pay, she would sit in a large overstuffed chair to divide her wages into piles. One pile was her church tithe; the other pile was for bills. Each week I could see her struggle to get enough money in the bill pile. I said, "But there is still money over here you haven't used." I learned that was God's money, and it could never be used for anything, except returned as the tithe.

On one of those Thursdays, I saw her struggling more than usual; there wasn't enough money for the bills. She finally stood up to put her tithe money in a church envelope. Then, she happened to look down and saw some money that must have fallen from the bill pile. Her explanation was God sent it to help pay the bills. We grew up knowing that money wasn't ours to use. I learned that lesson well, often calling on

God to help with my own bill pile.

Although I couldn't get help from my mother on school assignments, I did the best I could. One assignment was to develop an idea for the school science fair and to have our projects displayed in the library. I was so excited to make a solar system display, so I used papier-mâché and a coat hanger to make what I thought was a great project. I had used the science book picture of the solar system to form and label the planets. I used the coat hanger to hang the planets in their location to the sun. But as usual the other students had nicer looking projects.

When I had placed my solar system in the library for display, the teacher pulled me aside and told me that my project wasn't acceptable, but I could use the weekend to come up with another project before the judging on Monday.

The only book in our home was a Bible and the only other resource I had was the science book. I finally decided to build an irrigation system. I took a cardboard box, made piles of dirt to show the fields, colored strips of blue paper to show the water and little pine needles for the plants. I carried my project into the library on Monday morning and was on pins and needles, waiting for my class to go to the library to see the judges' comments.

In my young mind, I just knew I would get a good grade for what I had done. I looked for several minutes for my project and finally found it stuffed on the back of a shelf all crumbled, my project had not been good enough to display. I remember getting a grade of D for my work. I wasn't a great student, but that was one of the hardest grades I ever tried to digest.

At the age of 13, our house was purchased to make way for a new interstate highway. I had lived all those years in the same house at the end of a dirt road. I had my own special alone places for those solitude times. We relocated to a different town, although I was only four miles away, it was an entirely different, scary world. The school and the few friends I had known for years were now gone. A new school and new adventures lay ahead, but I was still a loner.

Now I didn't have my special place to withdraw to. The house was near the mill and they were so close together that we could hear our neighbors talking while in their own houses. I kept to myself and continued to struggle in school. I don't remember many of those few school years, except one.

In the ninth grade I had some wild idea that I could be a cheerleader. I wasn't aware that the selection would be determined by a popularity vote. I went to all the practices until one day we were told to get into teams. I wasn't asked to join a team, so I picked up my things and walked home. The other girls had grown up together … I was the new girl. The next day the sponsor asked why I left; I don't think she even realized I wasn't asked to join a team.

It was decided there would be no teams and the twelve

of us would perform the routine at the same time in front of the student body during a school pep rally. I nailed the routine even better than several of the inner circle girls. The next day the results were announced, but of course, I wasn't chosen. That was one of my first lessons that popularity matters in many areas, and I wasn't a popular girl.

At the age of 14, I was hired to dust the books at a local library during the summer break. I walked about two miles each way to the library and worked three days a week for about a month. The librarian was an older woman who needed someone younger to climb the ladder to reach the highest shelves. Working in the library was right up my alley, well in at least one way. I didn't have to do much talking.

One of those days, I had a seizure while dusting the books. The librarian wasn't familiar with seizures and became alarmed. I was sent home in a taxi and told that she couldn't let me work there any longer.

Although my first job had been cut short, I had saved the small earnings to purchase my first store-bought dress. There was a boutique within a few blocks of my mother's house, so I decided to go there to make this important purchase. I have never forgotten that dress. It was a light pink shirtwaist dress with twelve buttons down the front with a Peter Pan collar. I was sure that it was the most beautiful dress ever made.

Chapter 4

THE BREAKING POINT

Even though the abuse and my depression continued for years, it seemed easier when my angel was with me. I could close my eyes and talk to my angel. But by the time I was sixteen, I knew no one would be coming to rescue me.

I drove the 60 miles to see my father for one of the very last times. The visit was uncomfortable. I told my father that now I had a boyfriend, and I wouldn't be able to see him at Aunt Susie Mae's. I believe he knew I wasn't willing to allow the abuse to continue, but there was no mention of the "elephant" in the corner.

After that visit, I never had another seizure, but the severe migraines have continued my entire life. Although I have seen many specialists, the cause of the migraines was never discovered nor linked to the seizures.

I never dated much. Few guys even looked at me—a quiet girl wearing glasses. By the age of sixteen, attending school was a huge challenge for me. I found no joy in being a student. I knew I wouldn't continue. My family led me to believe it was a waste of time for me to stay in school and working in the mill was my direction in life.

I quit school after completing the 10th grade. In our small town, jobs were hard to come by, except at the mill. It seemed that the mill was always looking for workers. Having family members who were long-time employees made it even easier for me to be placed on a job at the same mill where my mother was working.

Somehow, during those first few months, I met a young man from one of the other small towns and dated him for about six months. We were able to come up with altered birth certificates, run off to a nearby justice of the peace and get married. Our ages would have required parental permission to marry, but with the altered certificates, there was no problem, and our parents didn't object and gave their approvals.

Before the end of our first year together, he decided to join the Navy. He wanted to see the world and escape our small town, while I stayed at home, worked, and waited for him to return. By our second anniversary, I sold all we had accumulated and took a three-day train journey to California. I had seldom left home and going across the entire country, I felt like I was really becoming an adult. We had little, but got by on just his military pay.

We set up housekeeping for about six months before his ship set sail, and I returned to live with my mother, only this time it was different; I was pregnant. My husband was able to come home on leave to be with me when our son was born. But after three days, he returned to his duty station.

When my husband's ship returned, my son and I made the trip back to California to live as a family. I tried several times to get a job. But with no experience, except from the mill, my options were limited. I remember interviewing for several jobs, even as a baby-sitter, but was told I had to have some kind of education. So I decided to enter the San Diego School of Nursing, where I was admitted into the Vocational Practical Nursing Program (VPN) without having to have a high school diploma.

In this school, I could attend class and progress at my own speed, and I could do my nursing internship in the evenings at a local doctor's office. I was able to complete the requirements and earned my VPN in about eight months.

My husband's tour of duty ended, and we moved back home. We left California before I had time to take the state VPN exam. I tried to use my new degree in a local hospital in town, but the state of Alabama only accepted Licensed Practical Nursing not VPN. I was told I could send my transcripts to the state board for review, but it was rejected. The school I had attended had lost its accreditation and my credits were useless. I would have to start my training all over again. But with the addition of another son and limited funds, I decided not to pursuit the degree.

Back home, my husband took a job as a police officer in a small town about forty miles from our families. I worked in a factory, sewing women's undergarments. My husband took care of the kids during the day when I worked, and I was with the kids when he worked nights. But I could see my husband was becoming different. He stayed gone for periods of time without reason, and even left our small boys unattended.

I was in the break room at the factory one day when a woman sitting at the table behind me started talking about her new boyfriend. She had stated that he was a police officer, and I could tell she was talking about my husband. I didn't say anything to the other woman, but that evening I asked my husband if it was true. He admitted it was. And the horror of a new "elephant" appeared. He was leaving me for another woman.

I had no choice but to return to my mother's house with my two small boys. What I had hoped would never happen to me—a divorce—did. The boys and I lived with Mother as I returned to work in the mill.

Going back to nursing school was out of the question, as I could hardly meet the needs of myself and my sons with just my limited income and no child support. I earned just enough money each week to pay for childcare and help Mother purchase groceries.

Finally, one day, I reached a breaking point. I gathered all the pills in the house, took them, and lay down to die. I felt I had let my sons and my family down, and my life was meaningless. But again, my angel wouldn't let me go; she stayed by my side for hours as I felt I was drowning, just wanting it to be over.

But again, I awoke with no noticeable injury. When I woke up, I wasn't even in a fog; my mind seemed to be clear. I believed my angel had been there to take care of me and give me the strength to live on. As I thought about what I had almost done, I realized my sons didn't deserve to be left without a father and mother. If my sons would have a better life than I had, I needed to make changes.

Out of the blue, or heavens, I decided to take the GED test. It took only one try for me to pass, but now what? I read in the local newspaper that a junior college was going to start teaching extension classes at local schools and churches, so I applied and was accepted—me, a college student.

The extension classes were miles from the main campus. I would have to take some remedial classes, but a general educational course would be my direction. For the first time in my life, I enjoyed being a student. I looked forward to classes and the knowledge I was gaining. I even looked forward to interacting with the other students and instructors. As is often the case with learning disabilities, some classes were difficult, but others easy. The difficult classes had to do with extensive reading, the easy ones with math. I was usually at the top of the class in my math courses and I was thrilled. I had found something I was really good at.

For the next two years, I took care of my kids, worked full-time, and took full loads at college. It seemed no time at all and I had completed the courses necessary for a degree. I remember going to the main campus on graduation day as much as if it was today.

Other than the birth of my children, I remember this day as one of the most joyful of my life. I can see the auditorium, the way the light fell through the tall windows. My family sat to the left and the sound of the Dean of Students' voice, as he called my name. My steps were shaky; I was trying to make sure I didn't stumble. I took that diploma in my hand. I held it close to my heart, fearing that it might break if I wasn't careful. I think I could even see my angel in the back of the room saying, "You go, girl!" An Associates' Degree in general education gave me the start I needed.

My family still couldn't say they were proud of me. They said I should stay at Mother's house and continue working in the mill. But I knew this was only the beginning of my pursuit of education. It took me about four weeks to apply for admission into the School of Education at Auburn University. I would study special education, a feeling I knew all too well.

My family continued to doubt my abilities and made my twenty-five mile compute from home to campus each day difficult. I knew if I was to stay in school, I would have to be totally dependent on myself. I received a couple of scholarships which paid for tuition, books and a small amount for living expenses. I loaded my sons into the car and moved to Auburn, Alabama.

I took a part-time job on campus between classes, making barely enough to support myself and my two sons. For two years, the boys and I struggled to just get by, no extras, but the boys never seemed to care. One of my son's was thinking about his upcoming birthday and had asked for a Bible. Again, my prayers went out, asking God to help me find the money. Within a couple of days of his birthday, a card came to me in the mail, unsigned, containing a ten dollar bill. I was able to buy his Bible and take the three of us out for twenty-five cent hamburgers to celebrate his birthday.

At the beginning of my senior year at Auburn University, a professor was recruiting students who would do their internship in South America. I wrote a paper about my interest and was chosen to go. The boys would stay with my mother for the three months I would be gone. I would live in the home of a family who had students attending the Pan American School in Bucaranga, Colombia.

Chapter 5

STUDIES ABROAD

The family in Bucaranga, Colombia, treated me like their own daughter. The father often sat with me during the evenings to talk to me about my interests. I had never known the feeling of having a father figure, who wanted to hear about what interested me. Every day, as I arrived home, I was met at the door by the housekeeper who had prepared a fresh bowl of bananas, pineapple and papaya, with no preservatives!

Often, as we sat down to eat dinner, the housekeeper would be given a handful of coins, and I would soon learn that at these times, she was being sent down the street to the market to purchase one pastry, for me. As often as possible, I would say in my limited Spanish, "too full" and would give the pastry to the children to share.

I tried as hard as I could to sample every new food and drink the family offered me. I had never been a coffee drinker, but that was their drink of choice. The coffee did taste a little better than I remembered from home and I was able to consume the drink.

Only on one occasion did the promise I had made to

sample all the foods seem too hard to keep. The father had called me to the table to discuss my day at school just before dinner was served. There in the middle of the table was a jar of what I was sure were eyeballs. They were spherical, the size of eyeballs, and I just know I saw blood shot veins on the surface. I had always known where my food came from, but this was different.

While I was trying to muster the courage to say, "no way" the father laughed and said they weren't what I thought they were. They were special onions he had a fondness for and wanted me to share his delicacies. Oh yea, I was also served chocolate covered ants and grasshoppers, and no they don't taste like chicken.

On a trip with some guys from the Peace Corps, we rode a bus to the end of the line and then walked three miles to a village that was very isolated. The village was small with about six houses along a gully. The houses were made of plaster with no doors or windows and dirt floors. The men were in the fields.

So with the help from our guides, we were able to talk to the women. One of the ladies brought us into her house where there were mats on the dirt floor and limited seating. Several of us would spend the time sitting on the floor. The hostess of this small group decided to make coffee for us. As one of the ladies was preparing the pot of coffee over the open flame, another lady ran to several of the huts to gather enough cups to serve their guests. We knew the sanitation conditions were probably not the best.

One of the members of our group, Paul, felt strongly against eating or drinking anything made at these huts. We reminded him it would be rude not to accept their hospitality, and we were probably using a large amount of their coffee supply. In a few minutes the ladies were bringing cups that were small, medium, cracked and stained.

When the coffee was handed out, Paul had been left without a cup and took a long sigh, thinking he had escaped the possible unsafe conditions. But they knew another lady who had a cup they could borrow. When one of the ladies returned to the hut and poured the coffee for Paul, we all had to hold our breaths to keep from laughing, as Paul was handed a cup three times larger than the ones we had been given. He had hoped he would get a small cup and could act like he was drinking, but now all eyes were on him, because he was the man of the group and was given the best cup for his coffee.

One morning as I was getting ready for school, I found a note on the bathroom door. It simply said, "No use." I went to the father to ask what the problem was. He told me there had been a landslide into the city's water source. There would be no public water for several days and to limit the flushing of the toilet. Our house had a storage tank on the roof for basic needs and bottled water for drinking and cooking; we would barely feel the situation.

As I rode to school that day, I saw the country's poor drawing water from the sewage ditch that would be boiled and made as safe as possible for their use. I knew there were many families who lived in cardboard huts who barely survived, but seeing them draw water out of the sewer was hard to imagine.

I had not often left the house after dark and had not seen the many horrible situations of the street children. But one evening, we were going to a special celebration and had walked a short distance. While we were walking, we came upon several children, perhaps five to seven years old, who were sleeping under the bushes, using newspaper as blankets in an attempt to stay warm. These were children the size of my own children, who were snug in their warm beds back home.

I was speechless as I was told by our escort not to bother the children. Another night at the house, the doorbell rang with some children calling out. When I asked the father what was being said, he translated, "Give us the bread that fell to the floor." When I asked why he didn't give them bread, he said that if he gave food to five children today, fifty children would come tomorrow. Having been raised in the rural south, I had seen the poor, but my heart went out to these "throw-away" children of Colombia.

The opportunity to live there was fantastic, and I was able to travel around the country of Colombia to see things I had only seen in books. A group who was interested in special needs children even offered me a job to return there after graduation to teach handicapped students. These were children of the elite, who were just left to be fed and kept comfortable. I missed my sons so much I couldn't think about moving so far away, even if the boys came back with me. It was such an unusual feeling to have people asking for my service, but I would finish my internship and complete my last semester of college.

But again, struggles would come. At the end of my second month in Colombia, I became very ill. I stayed in the Colombian hospital for a week before being released to return to the States. Another student would accompany me home to seek medical attention.

The diagnosis was type A Hepatitis. Perhaps it came from unsanitary conditions during our travels. I was given the option to go directly into isolation at the local hospital or to try and get better in isolation at Mother's house. Not having insurance, I chose Mother's house. My immediate family was given injections to abate the disease as I did all I could to fight my own illness. Each week I would go to the hospital for a blood test; each week I was told, "If your blood level doesn't improve, you'll have to go into the hospital."

As I fought my battle to get healthy, I knew my angel was with me night and day. There were days I barely had the strength to go to the restroom by myself. I stayed in Mother's house with a restriction sign on the door for about six weeks.

Finally, the blood levels improved, and I was told the disease was pretty much gone, but I would have reoccurrences of fatigue. I had six months left before graduation, and I wasn't going to let anything stop me.

I drove the car to campus, parked as close to my classes as possible and did most of my final assignments from bed with my boys bringing me whatever I needed.

In June, 1974, I was honored to be in the Auburn University's spring graduation to receive my Bachelors Degree in Mental Retardation. I did this for my boys, so they could have an example of what it means to, "Never, never give up!"

Chapter 6

FROM TEACHING TO ADOPTING

Those years were the beginning of special education laws, and the school systems looked for teachers to handle the challenged students. My first year as a teacher was in a very poverty stricken county. Although it wasn't a mill village, it was pretty much a dead-end for many students. I was assigned to teach high school special needs students who seldom had an interest in school or for that matter had a teacher who cared.

Of course, being fresh out of college, I thought I could save the world—one student at a time. The students not only were limited in book knowledge, but their ability to fit into the work force, as well. The possibilities of these young adults finding jobs would be limited.

My partner teacher was a five-year veteran, who said the county seldom did anything for these kids, even with textbooks on their reading levels. I invited a local reporter to visit our class and highlighted the need for on-the-job-training equipment. Within a matter of days the donations poured in, and we were able to equip a full kitchen, a hospital room and a small engine repair shop.

I wrote a manual called Vocational Access for Special Students (VASS), and begin teaching the students how they could gain usable skills for adult living after high school. My partner teacher taught the small engine shop and repaired donated equipment. I taught academics, as well as homemaking, cooking skills and simple home health care.

The principal allowed us to build a snack bar where our students sold snacks to the other students. We were able to use the money we earned to set up a salary system for them as they learned their skills. All of a sudden, the community was talking about the mentally retarded students at the high school.

My partner teacher and I decided to form a basketball team for our special needs students to compete in the Special Olympics. The students were not usually allowed to join sports teams in school because of their limited cognitive abilities and their behavioral outbursts. The boys were excited and willing to practice as much as possible to prepare. The teams won the first place at Regional Tournament, and we were going to the tri-state Special Olympics in Atlanta, GA. The students were both excited and anxious as we loaded the buses and headed out.

One of the students came to me about thirty minutes into the trip and said, "You see that hill back there? I have never been on this side of that hill." The students were wide-eyed with excitement. The boys were experiencing things they never thought possible.

We stayed in Atlanta for three days as they played in different heats, staying in the dorms at Georgia State University. The boys played hard, but were defeated in the last round of games. They were great and accepted their defeat with honor. They had enjoyed their adventure so much that being defeated wasn't even an issue. By the end of the school year, the students had increased by an average of two years academically.

At the beginning of May, as new assignments were being given for the next school year, I was called to the office to speak with the county school superintendent. I thought he would certainly tell me how proud the county was of my students' successes, but I was totally wrong. The superintendent held an elected position and with a business degree had no connection to education.

In the meeting, he discussed that my ideas of education were not in line with his expectations. He told me that I had a decision to make; I could accept a position with severely disabled students who "needed little more than baby-sitting" or I could resign. I was told that "the leaders of this community don't want to hear about that kind of students, the county's efforts should be placed on those students who will someday make us proud." I chose to resign from my first teaching position. My efforts had drawn criticism; I had taken wrong courses of action to save "throw-away" children.

As I wrapped up that first year and prepared to look for another teaching position, my ex-husband called. He wanted to see me. He had moved to Florida and had not seen the boys for the past three years. He asked if I could bring them for a couple of weeks to see him, and I agreed. The boys were excited to see their father and to go on a vacation. During the visit, my ex-husband asked me to forgive him for his adultery and asked if I would consider remarrying him.

During the past six years, I had often wondered what I had done wrong, and how I could have made things better for my husband. We remarried a month later, and life once again seemed good.

My husband and I became active in our new community, joined a church in the making and were at the church every chance possible. We even started our own bus ministry, visiting the neighborhoods on Saturday and returning on Sunday to take the kids to church with us. We purchased a house and attempted to form a good life there, but that too would change. My husband had lost his job in the construction industry, so we returned to Alabama to be near our family for support.

It appeared my husband was content with his family. He had gotten a good job at the local telephone company, and I was working at a local school. One Friday, we saw a program about children with special needs who were having problems being placed.

We chose a girl. Tamesha was four years old when she became a part of our family. She was just thirty days older than our youngest son, but she had the cognitive skills of a twelve-month-old child. Tamesha came to us with what we thought was deafness and mild retardation, but we soon learned she was deaf, mute, legally blind, had cerebral palsy and profoundly retarded. By the time the tests were in, she was already part of our family and a sister to our sons. When she came, she was unable to walk, still in diapers. She often sat banging her head on the floor and could eat only baby food.

Well, with three healthy brothers, she soon learned the joys and taste for many different foods. She no longer ate baby food. Tamesha didn't like marshmallows much, so if she had a sandwich cookie with marshmallow inside, she would eat both sides of the cookie and hand me back the marshmallow center.

On one of those early days, my sons and I held a summer learning program at our church for the neighborhood kids. About a hundred kids showed up each day. They were willing to read, do math, and hear Bible stories. We were usually at the church for four hours or more each day, and I often lay Tamesha down in the nursery to rest.

I went to check on her one day to find one of the troubled boys sitting in a rocking chair holding her. I watched for awhile, as he poured his troubled heart into singing her a song she couldn't hear.

Years later, he came to see me. He told me of the many bad choices he had made in his life, even drug use. As I listened and hugged him for several hours, I asked if he knew why I had never given up on him. He said he really didn't know. It was only then that I told him about seeing him sing to Tamesha years earlier. I told him that was the moment I knew he was a loving, caring person, even with his hard core. I also told him he had only needed someone who believed in his heart and knew he would come around.

Within six months, Tamesha was walking and potty trained. Although all the specialists told us she had limited cognitive skills, I do believe she could tell time. I would give her and her younger brother a nine o'clock bedtime; but about 8:50 each evening, she would get my attention and sign to be held. I would sign for her to come and sit in my lap. She would sit facing me with her legs on each side of me and her head on my shoulder. At nine o'clock, I would tap on her shoulder to tell her it was time to go to bed, but she would bury her face into my shoulder and giggle as if to say she wasn't ready.

My boys took her as their little sister growing to love, care for, and defend her as best they could. There were often stares and even unkind words by strangers. My youngest son was approached by a young boy one day saying, "If that was my sister I would give her away." My son never skipped a beat as he replied, "We're so lucky no one got her before we did."

In her foster home, she had been kept in a baby bed or playpen and was most comfortable staying within a four-foot square area. She would never get up from her play area or out of bed without first being given a sign. Even today, her comfort zone is a fixed area with no crowds or strangers as she sits quietly.

Tamesha was enrolled in a local elementary school; but the teachers weren't willing to deal with her outbursts, and I was often called from my classroom, 20 miles away, to remove her from school. We finally decided I should resign from my teaching position to better take care of her. I knew my husband's salary wouldn't be enough to fully support our family so I started "Dial a Maid," a house keeping service where I could work around her appointments.

When she was seven, the school system asked me to remove her, and I was able to get her into the Helen Keller Institute. She stayed there about fifteen months when I was called in for a conference.

In the short meeting, the staff explained that Tamesha had shown little progress and her acting-out-behaviors distracted the other students. They were requesting that we remove her from this school, too. I brought her back and reminded the local school district that they had to provide her with an education according to Public Law 94-142. She was placed in a class for severely disabled children without a sign language teacher, where she progressed very little.

One of the issues we had with the local system was a lack of transportation. Tamesha was daily released from school earlier than her brothers, so I enrolled her in an after school daycare center where she would stay until I could get home from my own school. I was told by the county transportation director that the system would not provide special transportation for her. The school bus would stop on the other side of a busy highway and she would have to get herself off the bus and cross the four lanes of traffic to her daycare, which was not in her cognitive or physical ability.

Well, time for mama bear to come out. I met with the school system and asked that they tell me the day they would start their transportation plan. Then I informed them that I would follow the bus; watch the driver put my severely handicapped child out on the side of the road, pick her up, and then, would spend his salary for the rest of her life. Well, somehow, after the meeting, the school system found a way to drop her off directly at the daycare center.

Chapter 7

VICTIM OF ABUSE

Another "elephant" was about to show its ugly head. My Mother's uncle passed away, and my sister and I drove with her some sixty miles out in the country for the family gathering. Mother knew how to get to Uncle Burl's house, but on our return it had gotten dark and we became lost.

To further complicate matters along the small county road, a tire on my car blew out; there was no spare, and we had no cell phone. This was in the '80's. I saw a small farmhouse a short distance off the road and walked to the house to look for help. It appeared that no one was home, so I returned to the car.

After about thirty minutes, a truck was pulling into the farmhouse driveway. I walked over to meet the man, his wife and young son, explaining what had happened. I asked if I could borrow their phone and phone book to find someone who might come out to fix the tire. There were a dozen or so names in the small book under tire repair. But you have to remember, we were in rural Alabama in the early evening on a Saturday, and there was not going to be any local Joe Bobs still working at a service station just waiting for the call. In fact, none of the calls were answered, and there was no AAA (American Automobile Association) nearby, either. I asked the man how far was it to the nearest open service station, and he said there was a 24-hour truck stop.

It was decided he would drive me to the truck stop to get the tire repaired while my mother and sister stayed with his wife and child at the farmhouse. The man and I set out in his truck toward the truck stop. I was wearing a white dress that day, and he was careful to spread a towel across the seat to protect my dress. It was already dark when we left the others and began to travel first along the two-lane highway.

The stranger began talking about how unhappy he was, and how he had decided earlier that day he would leave his wife; I was his answer to a new life. He began telling me how interested he was in me, and how much fun it would be if I would run off with him. It was such a shock to me to hear these comments coming from a man I had met less than an hour earlier.

He explained what a miserable life he had and just wanted someone to love him. As I listened, I tried to understand his situation without giving him false hope.

Before long, I realized the main road had become a dirt road. He had decreased his speed to barely moving. I couldn't understand how we were still heading toward the truck stop, but the minutes turned to hours.

Finally, after what seemed to be much longer, but was about two hours, we arrived at the truck stop. The tire was given to the attendant to repair as the stranger and I went into the café for coffee. I knew I was in trouble, but I didn't know what to do. I saw two state troopers in the corner having their late dinner and excused myself to go to the restroom, where I prayed some woman would come in, so I could send for help, but no one came.

About fifteen minutes passed before the stranger was knocking on the door telling me it was time to go. When I left the restroom, the troopers were gone. I was afraid to tell anyone what was going on, because I really didn't know how to get back to my mother and sister, and I was afraid the stranger would leave me and harm them. I didn't believe I could save myself, my mother and my sister if I refused to get back in the truck.

We were back on the road. After a while, we were back on the dirt road and then in a cotton field where the stranger stopped the truck. There was a quarter moon with clouds, which created a dark, scary night. There were no houses, no cars, just the stranger and me.

Several times he reached over to touch my arm, but I would gently take his hand and place it on the seat. He was telling me again how unhappy he was and just needed a new start. He even stroked my hair while telling me how beautiful I was. I tried not to let him know I was scared; I just listened to him, telling him how much I missed my kids and what a good life I had. I told him I was sorry that his wasn't good.

I remember keeping my right hand on the door handle to be able to run away, but I wouldn't know where to go. I didn't even know which direction to run through the darkness. I told him how worried my mother and sister would be and how much I really wanted to get back to them. I kept listening and talking, but I knew I didn't have the words; but my angel came to my aid with words to say.

After about three hours of sitting in the still darkness, he started the truck and drove through the cotton fields. Then, we were back on the county road. Perhaps ten minutes later, we were back at his house. It was hard for me to fight back my sobs when I saw my car.

My mother and sister rushed out of the house eager to get back in the car and head home. Mother thanked the stranger, and we set out following the directions he gave us to get back to the main road.

In about fifteen minutes, I pulled to the side of the road sobbing to my mother and sister that here is the truck stop we had gone to. A journey that had taken over five hours, now took only fifteen minutes.

The words I had spoken to the stranger came out of my mouth, but they were spoken by my angel. Those were words I could never had said on my own. However, my mother and sister had also felt the discomfort of being in the small farmhouse with the wife and child, which was far worse than anything I imagined I went through. I never called it a kidnapping—I was just held against my will. This was another experience to stuff in the corner with the "elephant," not to be mentioned again.

After six years, life with my husband became strained again. He often worked late and left early, seldom spending time with me or the children. He appeared to be going through the motions of being a husband and father, but with little connections. I'm not sure if too much of my attention was now being spent on having a special needs child, or my husband just had another itch, but he began to have another affair with a woman from his office.

The day I found out about the other woman, I begged him to give me another chance to be a good wife, to keep our family together. But he said he loved her more than me and just couldn't walk away from her. Instead, he walked away from me, now with four children and a limited income, as he went to start a new life. He filed for divorce a second time.

I cried a lot, wondering why I couldn't please him, or why couldn't I keep him interested in me. I had left my teaching job to be able to meet Tamesha's worsening daily needs, but now I had to accept that I couldn't adequately do both—care for her and provide the income I needed as a single parent, as well.

Because of Tamesha's growth, disabilities and the

local system's failure to adequately provide for her, I made the difficult decision to place her in a group home for special-needs adults, as I returned to teaching. I believed she would be better without me as I felt a failure for not being able to care for her.

The money from housekeeping had ended, and my teacher's salary had not started; we had little money for necessities. The child support from their father had not started. I remember having been someplace and returning home. I knew we needed money, but had too much pride to ask my family for help.

As we drove to the house, I told my oldest son to get the blue envelope out of the mailbox. He questioned how I knew a blue envelope would be in the box; I told him I believed God would provide for us. He was shocked as he reached in and pulled out the blue income tax refund envelope. There was enough money to purchase the items I needed to feed my children, until my teaching salary started.

Since most of my child-rearing years were as a single parent, I was often father and mother to my children. Their father started providing financial support after several months, but was short on emotional support. My ex-husband and his new wife even moved two houses down from us for about a year. Their father was building his new wife a grand new house in the country. But while living that close, he seldom had time to have his sons come for a visit.

Recently, my middle son reminded me of one of those tough, love times. We had a yard dog that was the responsibility of the boys to feed each day. Against my instructions, they often left the plastic cereal bowls in the yard with the food in it, which the dog quickly used as a chew toy and soon all the cereal bowls were gone. One morning as the boys came for breakfast, and there were no more bowls, I served their oatmeal to them directly on the table top. I bought new bowls, but none were left for the dog's chew toy again.

After a few months, I was dating a man whose mother was living in the same block as my mother, and we married a year later. By then, my oldest son had joined the Air Force and was on his own.

The first six weeks were really good, but soon another "elephant" appeared. My husband started slapping and punching me if I disagreed with anything he said. The first incident was as I was getting dressed for school, and he thought the dress I was preparing to wear was suggestive. He told me to change, and when I refused, he knocked me to the floor and tore the dress off of me, shouting accusations of my disloyalty. He later apologized saying he didn't mean to hit me and it wouldn't happen again.

However, experience has proven that once a man has put his hands on you in anger, there is going to be more abuse. I soon learned to get his approval each day for the outfits I prepared to wear. I had enjoyed baking and sharing desserts with my co-workers, but that too brought his anger, so I stopped baking for others. He controlled everyplace I went and who I saw, even my family. I lived in constant fear of what he might do next.

Another time, I was preparing to be a chaperone for my son's school marching band contest trip. That morning, as I was getting ready, he told me I couldn't go, that my place was at home. I reminded him that the two younger children would be with their father; he would be working the 4:00 to midnight shift, and I could be back home before he got off work. But I knew from my husband's voice, that I would not be allowed to accompany the band.

The band trip was very special for my son; he had been chosen by the band director to be the drum major for the band at the contest, and he could win a gold medal. I took my son to the school to meet the other students and saw the buses leave for the trip. He had worked hard on his music and enjoyed being a leader.

That night, as he led the band in their performance; my son won his gold medal. But I wasn't there to cheer him on or rejoice with him about his scores. Other parents were there to congratulate my son on leading the band to a gold medal.

When I returned home that morning, I knew my husband would be there alone, but I thought he had gotten past being angry since I had done what he told me to do.

When I returned home, I entered the house and went directly to our bedroom.

The house was unusually quiet; no TV, radio or voices. I entered the bedroom not knowing my husband was hiding behind the door. I'm not sure what he hit me with, but I fell backwards. My left arm wedged between the mattress and the bed railing. As I lay there stunned, he jumped on me with his full weight, with his knee buried in my left thigh. I couldn't move or barely hear, but I remember these words, "Die, d@#* you, die."

The first few seconds, I tried to fight him off, but I knew he was choking the life out of me. I was only seconds from death when we were startled with a presence in the room, and I knew my angel was there. I lay on the floor unable to move, gasping to breathe. I could hear him in the den, putting shells into his gun. He came back into the room, holding the shotgun to my head and said, "You tell anyone about this or call the police, and I will kill you and your kids."

I felt the tone in his voice was a promise he intended to keep. I knew when he left the house for work, but I lay in a heap unable to make sense of what had happened. As the day turned to night, I finally got myself off the floor and into the shower, feeling the water sting the abrasions.

I stayed home doing my best to clean the house and do all the things a good wife should do to please her husband. I felt I was the cause of the abuse and needed to keep trying to do better.

After several other incidents and fearing for my life, I decided to tell my mother about the abuse. Her response was, "The Bible says a wife must submit herself to her husband. You need to listen to your husband and do whatever he tells you."

The only person I felt would be there for me turned her back, and I was left to handle the abuse on my own. For three years, I felt I had no one else to turn to and was beaten down in every way possible. I lived with daily sexual, physical, and emotional abuse; he was always sure when the abuse started that no one else was in the house, and that I had no proof of the abuse, which of course, I thought I deserved.

I lived two completely different lives. At school, I tried to be upbeat and cheerful, but I knew as soon as I got home, I could never discuss any activities from school or people I talked to. Regardless of the weather, I often wore a turtle neck and long sleeve shirts to cover the bruises. My body began showing the constant abuse, and I was accused of extreme dieting by my family.

There was one more incident that was to occur, but it wasn't against me. My youngest son didn't like riding the school bus, and his stepmother had offered to let him ride to school with her son. I told him he could stop riding the bus and start riding with her. My husband followed me into the laundry room that day saying I should have discussed it with him before making a decision. For the first time in five years, I stiffened myself and said, "No, you aren't picking on my son." He went to hit me; I grabbed his hand and said, "This is it, if you hit me again, you better be sure I die. Because if not, I'm coming after you with all the strength I have, and then I'm reporting your abuse to the police." He pushed me away saying, "You aren't even worth killing."

It was the weekend starting spring break, and the small kids would be staying with their father and step-mother. I arranged for my middle son to stay with a friend. I packed a bag, and left during the night while my husband was at work.

After two days, I called and told him I wanted him out of the house; and if he didn't go, I would report the abuse. It took a couple of days for him to remove his property. I stayed away, checking the driveway a couple of times to see if his truck was gone.

Finally, I thought it was safe to return. I knew I was going against what my family thought I should do, but I knew I had been willing to take the abuse myself, but not when he turned it on my son.

But the "elephant" didn't go away. Even though the house had belonged to me before our marriage, I had refinanced it, and put his name on the paperwork.

On a regular basis over the next eight months, he came into the house taking whatever he wanted. I asked the police for a restraining order to keep him away, but I was told it was as much his house as mine, and he could return until the judge decided whose property it was.

I listened at night for unfamiliar noises. I would try to stay awake, but often fell asleep in the early hours. On three occasions, I awoke with him standing over me. He said, "I am clocked in at work, and no one knows I'm gone. I can kill you anytime I want to and will never be blamed."

He stalked me night and day for months. When I left home in the morning, he was waiting outside; he followed me to school and sat outside until I left in the afternoon; he followed me almost everywhere I went. There wasn't a moment during those months that I could let my guard down. He was so obsessed with stalking me that he lost his job, which just gave him more time to watch me. As each day turned into night, my fear level intensified; always listening for unfamiliar sounds, watching the shadows.

Finally, our court date arrived. We were on the list to have our case heard. But after waiting about six hours, my attorney told me the judge was closing for the day, and our hearing would be scheduled again in a few weeks.

I guess if it were now, I would have been arrested or shot for my next move. I burst into the judge's chambers demanding to be heard. He told me I had to leave; that he couldn't hear me at this time, but I told him I had something to say first. Then my husband, his attorney, and my attorney had entered the judge's chambers. I remember telling him about the stalking and threats my husband had been making, then in the presence of the four men I said, "You won't help me; I'll have to help myself. My son has given me a shotgun and shells. If my husband comes into the house again, I will do my best to kill him, and then you all will have to explain to my family how you failed me."

The judge looked at me and again told me I had to leave. I left the courthouse, but fully expected I would have to carry through on my promise. However, would you believe my husband never entered the house again? Even so, I still kept the gun and tire iron under the bed for months.

Because of the trauma I had experienced, every night continued to be a struggle. I had my youngest son at home and I knew it was my responsibility to protect him. I rearranged our bedrooms adjoined by a door, installed deadbolt locks and slid a chest to block the entryways every night. But still I grew to fear the night. I often woke gasping for breath, feeling I was falling into a deep well that never ended. I wanted someone to reach out and grab a hold of me to stop my fall, but no one came. The darkness inside the well was all I could see. My life was in despair, and I blamed myself. For months, I could only sleep facing an open doorway, with my arm positioned across my throat for protection.

Chapter 8

A NEW "ELEPHANT"

Tamesha stayed in the state school and graduated. She is now in her mid-thirties and works in a sheltered workshop. She lives in a group home with other adults; but she still doesn't like change, and she would rather stay at home than go out of her comfort zone.

Both my older sons joined the military and married, leaving just my youngest son and me at home. Living in a broken home is difficult for most children, especially boys. My son had gotten distant, spending most of his time in his room.

One night he seemed stressed. I tried to talk to him, but he didn't want to listen to me. He said, "What would you do if I slapped you." It took me a few seconds to sense he was serious. I had not allowed the boys to see the violence I had endured; I couldn't believe he was asking me this question.

I said, "Well, if it happens, I would knock you to the floor, stomp on you, call the police, have you arrested and sent to juvenile hall. But let's just wait to see if my answer might change if that ever does happen." He has never raised his hand against me, but decided that it would be best to leave me and live at his father's house. I knew I had raised my sons with a strict hand, and perhaps I was too hard. But seeing what I see now, the strictness paid off as my three sons are honorable men with families of their own.

I started a group in our small town called Christian Singles. The group was formed for unmarried adults to find ways to socialize with others. I organized cookouts, dining out, movies, Bible study groups, and ice cream socials. Our weekly meeting place was a local non-denominational church.

One night, one of their church members decided to join our group. I had not thought about getting involved again, but forty-five days later we were married. I felt I could finally see out of the top of the well.

The Monday following our wedding, a new school year began, and as many systems do, all the school system's staff had gathered in the high school auditorium for a pep talk. It was during this meeting that I was called to the stage and honored as the Teacher of the Year for the system.

As the assistant superintendent started describing the person who had been chosen, I kept thinking, "Could it really be me?" When my name was called, I felt I had finally made the big times in my profession. I tend to shy away from public recognition, but this time I was thrilled.

As I looked out at the other educators who had gathered, I wondered if they really knew how far I had come.

And if they really knew the real me, would I still have been chosen.

Later, when I called Mother to tell her the news, she could only say how nice that was. She still couldn't muster the words to say she was proud of me. But everything else was good, and I was embracing my new, wonderful life. My husband was a college educated man, well versed in the Bible, and treated me like a queen. He was all I had ever hoped for. We even joked about growing old together and having wheelchair races down the nursing home halls. He was my best friend; we gladly spent every possible moment together. It was as if we were both trying to make up for time lost.

On one particular sunny day, a friend and I were driving down a busy four-lane road. To the left and right of us the roads intersected with our street; there was no traffic light. The cars traveling to my left had been at a standstill for several blocks; however, my lane was moving steadily. I had no reason to slow down or stop and was probably traveling 40-45 miles an hour.

We were just chatting about our day, not even thinking about what might happen in the traffic. Out to my left, a driver had decided to stop, which only gave one cars' length of space in the traffic for another driver, but that driver decided to move into that gap and sped across all four-lanes of traffic. They were coming right toward my friend and me.

When I saw the car, I knew I had no hope of avoiding

the collision. My friend and I both screamed. I watched the other car reach the very front of my car—thinking, "Would I survive the crash?" But then, it was gone. No collision, nothing stopped our car, there was just no car.

It took a few minutes for us to realize that a miracle had just happened. My angel had removed the car from the scene. I wondered how the driver of the other car felt when it seemed his car had a tailwind that took it a block down the street in the blink of an eye. And again, I was reminded—I still had a purpose for being here.

We were married several years. During that time, my husband got and lost many jobs. I knew he was smart and could do many things, but I didn't understand why he kept losing jobs. Some of the jobs were for just days, while others were for a few months.

He had told me that depression ran deep in his family; his mother had taken her own life about twenty years earlier; his grandmother spent most of her life in mental institutions; one brother had a drinking problem that lead to his death, and his younger brother lived with little contact with others. I could see his depression often, but I thought he had it under control. I was the only one who knew of his demon.

I came home one day to find him totally distraught, sitting on the sofa, weeping. He explained to me that he had served two and a half years in federal prison and was now on the national sexual offender registry. He had failed to register since we married, and he feared he would soon be arrested to serve out the rest of his five-year sentence.

He told me that his ex-wife and her connected family had framed him, but he was innocent of those crimes. I didn't ask any questions of him. He went into little detail, but I could tell he would not survive going back to prison. I totally believed him and still do to this day. I never feared for the safety of my children, grandchildren, or myself.

The next day he registered with the local authorities and didn't return to prison. I didn't know in the beginning that his "elephant" would affect me in every possible way.

Chapter 9

BEST TEACHER AWARD

After I was chosen Teacher of the Year, doors began to open for me in my career. I enrolled in the Auburn University doctorial program in educational leadership. As I took classes to complete the requirements, I decided to split from the doctorial program and pursue the specialist in education track to avoid having to write the dissertation. I took the same classes as if I was getting a PHD, but I just didn't want to do the extensive writing because I felt incapable of doing it.

Within two years, I earned one of the highest degrees that were offered by Auburn University, an Educational Specialist in Educational Administration and Leadership. What wonderful doors had opened for me when I decided to "Never, never give up."

I wrote several grants, which helped me to earn funding to write and publish two workbooks for national and world geography for special needs students. In the grants, I received funding to have cement slabs poured on the playground where I drew the United States and World maps. This allowed the students to have a better understanding of their relationship with the States and other countries as they used my work books.

The first workbook for the United States gave brief descriptions of each state and a small fun fact. For the world workbook, I selected several countries to highlight; giving demographic information, recipes and simple games the local children would have played. The workbooks were printed and distributed to local schools.

Other honors were coming my way; Innovative Teacher of the Year for Chattahoochee Valley, Outstanding Georgia Citizen, National Professionally Recognized Special Educator Award, Georgia Distinguished Service Award, The National Council for Exceptional Children Excellence in Teaching, Soroptimist International Woman of the Year Distinction in Education, The Gateways Educator of the Year, Smithsonian/State Farm Innovative Teacher, and President of the GA Council for Exceptional Children.

The President of GA CEC was a volunteer position, but the council members gain much recognition for their work by having the opportunity to travel locally, state and even nationally. My husband often went with me and was accepted by the other council members. He often sat in business meetings, but never spoke out.

At one of these meetings, he became offended at some of the council member options about my efforts and decided to set them straight. He waited until we returned home, and I had gone to sleep. Then he wrote letters to each of the council stockholders.

When I awoke the following morning, he had already gone to the post office and mailed the letters. Then he shared with me what he had written. He set about to tell the members how far off track they had become and demanded that most all the council members be asked to resign. This was a position I had worked so hard for, but now felt my husband's words would be a barrier to any good my continued involvement might bring. I was so embarrassed after reading the letters he had written that I wrote a letter of apology and submitted my resignation.

Within months, my husband was job-hunting again. He was interviewed and hired by a large non-profit organization about forty miles from home. It was decided we would sell our home, buy a house near his office, and I would look for a new teaching position.

I was offered a position in one of the poorest neighborhoods in the county, where neither kids nor their parents had much interest in learning. Because of my innovative nature, I stepped out of the comfort of my classroom to involve other students and teachers, the administration, and the local share holders into the world of the disabled.

One of the first things I did was to engage my students into the World Olympics that was coming to Georgia. I researched and found the names of over 200 countries whose athletes would be participating in the games. I found pictures of their flags and basic demographic information. I drew off the flags, printed the basic information on the reverse, and instructed my students how to color the flags. We displayed the finished flags crisscrossing our hallway. I often left our classroom door open so my students could hear the kind remarks that were made by the other students and teachers when they saw our flag display.

I went a step further, and with the help of my German-born teacher's assistant, I held a Germany Day. I made matching aprons and skirts for the girls, vests for the boys, and with my limited drawing skills, I drew a traditional German village on our classroom walls. I invited other teachers, school and county administrators, city and county officials, as well as Olympic leaders, to our Germany Day Lunch.

Many of the dignitaries had never even visited this small neighborhood school. My assistant and I prepared several authentic German dishes, including schnitzel and Black Forest Cake. My son and daughter-in-law were stationed in Germany at that time, and they provided authentic German candy to share.

We had about 65 visitors that day as our students proudly served as greeters, escorts and servers; they were thrilled with their new found recognition. Those who participated with us were almost as excited as we were with the results and the appropriate behaviors of our special needs students.

Later that same year, the school principal approached our class to create a program in recognition of Earth Day. Again, my main focus would be to get my special needs students and their parents involved.

Many parents felt their limited academics had left them unable to participate in school activities. But I knew if we were to make a difference, not only in the students in my class, but the school and the community, we would need to come together with an innovative plan.

My plan would be based on the idea of recycling to help save the Earth, one aluminum can at a time. I developed and sent out flyers, telling the students, teachers, parents and community leaders that we would be collecting aluminum cans.

The idea would be for all the school's students to bring the cans to school; my students would go to the classrooms first thing in the morning, bring the cans to our class, count them, and record the numbers on a chart. The students would then bag and help me take the bags of cans to the local recycler.

I only drove the truck; the students unloaded the bags on the conveyor belt and watched the cans, as they were weighed and crushed before they were given a pay slip. The students took the pay slip to the window and received cash for our load of cans for the day. When they returned to school they had to fill out a deposit slip to put the money into the school bank, and within days the "Helping Save the Earth One Can at a Time" began to spread.

Parents, friends and neighbors started bringing first bags of cans; then it increased to trunk and truck loads. Parents who never felt they could support their children were coming to school. They were offering to help count, chart and deliver the cans. My students were using this project to learn their math and reading lessons, as well as geography and science. My students were seen as lucky to be in that special class.

Within 2 months, the program had recycled enough cans to earn over $2,000.00 for the school's special projects. The principal was so impressed he asked that we continue the project for the entire new school year. We would start an individual student recognition program, where each student who brought 100 or more cans would be a "Student Recycler."

As the project developed, more and more parents were getting involved. On a regular basis, we were earning between $500-$800.00 each month, which we used to beautify the school and neighborhood. The special needs students included the planting and maintaining the gardens around the school in their daily academics. The students were so proud of their work; they were often standing in front of the school at the end of the day, protecting their flowers.

A large neighborhood business became involved as a sponsor. They had their own workers pour the foundation and erect a green house on the school grounds. There the students were taught to plant seeds and raise their own plants. Larger beautification projects involved parents and community volunteers, and for the next two years, the school received local and state, "Keep Georgia Beautiful" awards, which included two Georgia Schools of the Year. I was presented with a "Keep Georgia Beautiful" Teacher of the Year Award.

I enjoyed my assignment with difficult kids who others wouldn't work with. Most cases were positive, but I encountered several extreme behaviors as I was called to defuse situations, remove knives, guns, and other weapons.

Two of those students were twin brothers, Ronnie and Donnie. If I alone had made the placement decision, it would have been severely, socially maladjusted, rather than emotional/behavioral disorders. The second diagnosis is what would give the boys protection and allow them to remain in the public school system.

After two years of trying to modify their behavior, it was apparent that these boys were going to do whatever they wanted to do, regardless of the consequences. Both of these boys had served time in juvenile detention facilities, with no apparent improvement.

The boys were in the eighth grade. They stood about 6'3" and were muscular. No other students at school were willing to confront them. When the twins moved from class to class, the other students gave them a wide berth; no one wanted to be accused of getting in their way.

Chapter 9

On one occasion, a student pushed into Donnie and a shoving match began. Ronnie quickly came to his brother's side, and a fight broke out. It took five or six adults to get Ronnie and Donnie off the other student, as they continued to kick the fallen boy. Ronnie was taken off the hall, as I was left to escort Donnie into a nearby classroom. I spoke quietly, with calming words to try and settle the animal fire within him.

As Donnie became aware that the police were coming, he began to accuse me of taking sides with the other student. I told him I didn't know how the fight had started, but I did know he and Ronnie had taken the opportunity to inflict greater injury to the other student than was necessary.

Donnie continued to pace the floor until the police arrived, and two officers handcuffed him and prepared to take him from the classroom. He lurched forward, head-butting me, bursting my lip open. Before the officers could get him out of the room, Donnie said, "I know you work late, I know how to get into this building, even when you think the doors are locked, and you're dead." I leaned forward and whispered, "I'll be waiting for you, bring it on."

Donnie and Ronnie were found guilty of assault and violation of their parole. They were sentenced to finish their time at the juvenile detention center, plus another two years.

After that, I tried to be mindful during late-night work-sessions, and I always carried a radio while I was still in the building, especially as I walked the building to check and see that the other doors were locked before I left for the night. One of the janitors, George, was always there and would stop by my office to check on me.

As I made the rounds to check the doors one night, the main lights had been turned off, but there was enough light for me to get to the doors and return. About half way down the hall, I heard noise coming from one of the classrooms and called out to George on the radio, but got no answer. My instinct was to walk as fast as possible the other way, but I had a job to do and I was going to do it. As I used my pass key to enter the room, I saw a figure in the shadows and flipped on the lights, scaring Miss Wells, the classroom teacher as much as she scared me. No one had known she had been spending nights in her classroom because of financial problems. She was between apartments.

In just a minute, George was there, saying he was outside the building when he heard my call and had already called the police. We were all eager to meet the police and tell them it was a false alarm. After that night, Miss Wells found a place to live, and George made sure to walk with me for door checks.

Another incident that could have turned serious was with a female student. I again was working with at-risk youth. This time it was in an all girls' school. I was walking down the hall, minding my own business, when I heard screaming come from the principal's office.

As I reached the door, a student rushed past me. The principal yelled, "She has a knife and is going after a teacher. Stop her!" There were times when I was indeed a runner, but I didn't think that this was going to be one of those days. I was in a business suit, wearing high heels.

First, I kicked off the shoes, lifted my skirt a little and set out running to catch the knife-wielding student. I caught her from behind in a bear hug, which left her arms a lot freer than I had wanted. She stabbed right as I leaned left several times until the principal and janitor caught up with us and took the knife from her hands.

I was about to release my hold when the principal said, "Don't let her go; the police are on the way." Well, I tried to keep in shape, but here is a teenage girl pumped up on adrenaline, who did not want to be held. And here was a middle-aged woman, who had just sprinted further than she had wanted to run.

I was able to wrestle her into an empty classroom, as she was telling me I couldn't keep her there. But by then, my own adrenaline was pumping. I said, "We are on the second floor. If you want to leave, your only choice is out that window." I leaned against the door and waited for the police to arrive.

Whenever these situations occurred, I seemed to be able to handle the violence when other educators couldn't or wouldn't, and I was more than eager to attempt to save these individuals who others viewed as throw-away students.

Chapter 10

DEATH OF A LOVED ONE

In the summer of 1999, I received an overwhelming honor. Because of the program I had developed in the small community school of recycling aluminum cans, I was chosen and named one of twelve teachers in the United States and Canada as the Innovative Teacher of the Year by State Farm Insurance and The Smithsonian Institute. I was honored in Washington, D.C., for several days of events and parties and was featured in several magazines, including *National Geographic* and *U.S. News and World Report*.

I was shocked one day to receive a phone call from my son, who was serving in Korea. He had picked up a magazine and saw an article about his mother. This award gave me notice in the district as I continued to serve the special needs students. For several years I chose not to use my Educational Specialist in Educational Administration and Leadership Degree as I was excited about the projects I was developing for these students.

After five years with the non-profit organization, my husband's depression took over again, and he quit his job. I took on two part-time jobs to help with our financial obligations. He was out of work for months, too depressed to even look for a job.

During this time, my 90-year-old mother had developed fears about living alone and voiced her desire to move in with us. As an adult, I had developed a close bond with my mother.

For the past twenty years, I had gone to her house, and then apartment, every Saturday morning. Then we would spend an hour or so at the beauty shop, go for breakfast, and end up shopping. Friends and family knew if they needed either of us, we would be together. I had reached a point in my life where many of my childhood fears were gone, and I loved spending time with her. The thought of her living with me would be a great, joyful time for us.

I contacted my brother with the news of Mother's wishes, and he just said he would get back to me. He had not shared with me that he had reservations about her living with me. My brother, sister and I had always said that we wouldn't let Mother live her final years in a nursing home. We would provide care for her in our homes.

A few weeks later, my brother informed me that he alone decided the best place for Mother would be a nursing home. Because we didn't have a father figure in our lives, when my brother became of age, my mother always asked him to make decisions for her. Now he was determined to change the rules. Since my brother had a closer relationship with my sister than I did, she agreed with whatever he decided to do. Not wanting to awaken her own "elephant," Mother wouldn't go against my brother, so she went along with his decision to place her in a home.

In December, 2002, Mother entered the nursing home, but within three days she was near death. She had contracted a staph infection and had given up on life. When the family gathered at the hospital, my husband voiced his desire to take Mother home with us. My brother's new wife reported that my husband wanted to take Mother out of the hospital against the doctor's approval, which was never his intention.

Two days later, my brother had a temporary injunction making himself guardian for our mother and continued his plans to have her remain in the nursing home. Mother began to improve, but now she was begging to go home with me. I told her she had agreed with my brother to live in the nursing home, but she said if I would take her home, she would voice her desires. I had never gone against my brother or sister in any family matters.

Over the years, when I didn't agree, I just remained silent. Both of them lived further away than I did, and for many years I had taken care of whatever she needed. I tried to talk to my brother again about her staying with me, but he just wouldn't listen. He had made the decision and wasn't willing to back down. My sister had moved away and would visit Mother only once or twice each year. She didn't seem interested in the war that had developed. Deep down inside, I just knew sending Mother to a home wasn't in her best interest.

I hired an attorney to begin the process to have her declared competent to make her own decisions. It took almost a month for a competency hearing to be set for Mother. My sister didn't visit Mother during those weeks at the home, and my brother only visited three to four times. But I wanted to be there for her, so I worked my regular school shift, plus a four-hour tutoring position, and traveled the 90-mile round trip to spend time with her each day. About four weeks later, a hearing was held. The case went before a jury of retirees at the county courthouse. My brother and sister spoke of my troubled marriages and felt that I wasn't dependable.

Mother was too upset about my brother's actions and would not speak at the trial. After a short deliberation, the jury over turned my brother's injunction and gave my mother back her own decision-making powers. Her first words were to ask if I would take her home with me.

After the hearing, my brother, sister and their children stormed out of the courthouse, telling Mother she had made her decision on who she really loved. I made attempts often to involve my siblings in family events, but they refused to attend. I sent holiday cards that were often returned to me unopened. Christmas was the only time they made an effort to have Mother for a visit.

My sister and I had never been close. She was much older than I was and we just didn't connect. I remember one time when she was mad at me she remarked, "I have hated you since the day you were born." I could only reply, "But being born wasn't my fault."

When Mother moved in, we included her in trips, church, dining in nice restaurants, and even the symphony. These were cultures she had not been exposed to, but learned to appreciate. We made a place on the back patio where she would enjoy lying on an old country swing to take naps. We arranged for Meals on Wheels to bring her lunch, and she even loved that part of her days.

Some days, she felt like cooking, and we gave her free reign of the kitchen. Other days, we let her do what part she could. She so much enjoyed the fun times we were having. When I came in each evening from work, she would be in her bedroom watching TV, waiting for me to come in and tell her about my day. I would lay across her bed as we talked before dozing off for short naps. We both looked forward to and loved those short mother-daughter talks. Mother appeared to really enjoy living in our home and things were great for about two years.

But the mother I had known just two short years earlier was now no longer the woman who was living in my home. She had gotten hateful, telling us that family members were stealing from her. She stopping leaving the house with me, fearing I would take her to a nursing home against her wishes. Soon, Mother began having signs of dementia, making comments to her sister about our lack of care. One particular weekend, Mother complained that we were withholding food and medical care, and she became severely agitated.

For the first time in my life, I shouted angry words at my mother—words that still trouble me today. My brother's son had stayed in contact with me, even though his father didn't. He often visited Mother and updated her on what was happening with the others. Unsure what I needed to do for Mother, I called him, asking him to allow Mother to stay with him for a few days so she might calm down. He and his family had fallen on hard times, and I hoped the funds I could provide him would benefit the family, as well as he could give me a respite.

Within two days, my brother found out that my mother was with my nephew, and he removed her from there and took her to his house. For several months, Mother lived with my brother, but the dementia worsened. My sister-in-law believed that all old people were useless and needed to be put in a home. Finally, my brother arranged to place Mother back in the nursing home. Her emotions and state of mind seemed to change in minutes. I knew this time I wouldn't be able to take her back home with me; I was going to have to leave her in the home. Mother stayed in the home about five months, hating every moment of her stay. Every time I went to visit, I left in tears, feeling guilty for not doing more to keep her with me. Finally, the shell of my mother gave up, and she died at the age of 95. I believe a broken heart quickened her death.

Funerals and memorials were an important part of my mother's life. Perhaps, ten years earlier, Mother had prearranged her funeral. She chose and paid for her casket and the entire arrangements. In Mother's red metal box were important papers, including her funeral arrangements. She had specific music and speakers she wanted to be there for her.

The days before and day of the funeral were filled with turmoil. I had not seen or spoken to my brother or sister for the three years since the competency hearing. Knowing my husband and brother were at odds, I went into the funeral home with my daughter-in-law to meet my brother and his wife to make Mother's final arrangements. My sister decided not to join us, but would agree with whatever my brother decided. But my brother and sister-in-law had developed their own plans, going against the list in her red metal box.

During the meeting I asked my brother to use some of the desires mother had expressed prior to her dementia, but he refused. He and I had grown up with no violence in Mother's house and few words were spoken in anger. Never would I have believed my brother's next actions. When I asked again that her pastor be allowed to conduct the services, he rose to his feet and charged at me while his wife yelled, "Slap the b**ch."

For the first time in sixty years, my brother slapped me. The hurt was so much deeper than the burn to my face; my heart was breaking. I could barely stand or speak. Through sobs and disbelieve I expressed that he could do the funeral his way. I would arrange a memorial service to be held at her church with her desires of music and the long-time pastor the way she would have wanted.

I limited myself as much as possible to visitation at the funeral home; I knew Mother would not like seeing a disruption. My sister, brother and their families arranged the family activities, but excluded me and my children. I attended the funeral service, but sat in a side room, again, not wanting a disruption.

Later that day at Mother's home church, a memorial service was held with many of her friends and the long-time pastor remembering her life. The day after her funeral, I saw my Mother's vision one final time. When she appeared she said, "I didn't have a chance to say 'Good-bye,' and I wanted to say 'I love you.'"

My sister and brother completely removed themselves from any contact with me. Because of the anger during those days and my husband's own difficulties, I was not allowed to mention my mother, brother or sister in our home. It felt like I was never allowed to grieve for her and another "elephant" entered my life.

As the days crept by, I also became depressed and wondered where to turn. I just knew I wasn't ready to just give up. I decided it was time to use my last degree and look for leadership roles. At the same time, my husband decided to look for work again. He had an interview with a small company that needed a bookkeeper. They needed to run a security report first; then he received a call withdrawing the job offer because of his criminal background.

But the report didn't end there. The HR director sent my husband's report to the superintendent of the school district. I put my resume in the local school system leadership pool, but wasn't getting any attention.

In a private meeting, I was told I would never be offered an administrative position with the school system because of my husband's record. I was further told that he was never to set foot on any school property. I felt the full weight of his conviction coming down on my heart.

We spent several days crying together, wondering what to do. I thought about leaving education for good, so I took a couple of months off to throw myself a pity-party. However, somewhere along the way I remembered my own motto to, "Never, never give up." When my self-imposed pity-party was over, it was time to stand and keep moving.

Chapter 11

"NANNA"

I started sending resumes to other than those ordinary school systems, mostly to charter schools. Out of the heavens, because I don't remember sending this resume, I received a call to interview at a small college in west central Georgia. I went to the interview, not expecting to be considered for the position. I was swept off my feet and was treated as if I was the leader they had been looking for. I was assured I was at the top of the applicant list and would receive a call soon.

Just a couple days later, in the vegetable section of the local supermarket, I answered my cell phone to be asked if I would join the faculty of Georgia Southwestern State University as their Dean of Early College. This was a program where start up money would be funded by the Bill and Melinda Gates Foundation. I would be given half a million dollars to set up and run a school for at-risk students.

I had about three months to research other schools. I visited schools in Boston and New York, set up a selection process, developed the academic program with state guidelines, found books, and hired staff. I spoke on TV and radio programs and went to a dozen or so schools to talk to their rising 9th graders.

With information from the Gates Foundation, I was able to develop criteria that might determine if a student was, in fact, close to dropping out of high school. When students had been interviewed, fifty were invited to join our first Early College class. The University President and Vice President of Academic Affairs, who had written the original grant, were totally on board. They had given us the first floor of the education building for our offices and classrooms and were visiting the students at every chance possible.

I was able to find a counselor, English, history, science, and PE teachers, and an administrative assistant fairly easily. However, I wasn't able to find a math teacher. On one occasion, while talking with the VP of Academic Affairs, I expressed my concern. I told her my son had just retired from the Air Force, was moving to town, had a degree in international business, and wanted to pursuit his second career in teaching. She took it upon herself to contact the GA Board of Regents to get permission to offer him a probational teaching certificate. So, now I had the entire staff ready to start the first school year of GSW Early College.

This was my dream job—a position that I had only allowed myself to daydream about. But this joy also came with the great fulfillment of my son, who wished to relocate near me. He had served the Air Force for 22 years and was away from home almost all of those years. Not only did I have this great career opportunity, but my son was home, too. The development of the GSW Early College was the most exciting, fulfilling years of my entire thirty-three educational career.

The school was also what many of the at-risk students needed. They were excelling, wanting to be in school each day. The parents were reporting how excited their children were about their education for the first time since elementary school. One of my granddaughters joined the school the first year, and another granddaughter came the second year. I always wanted the staff and students to know that although my son was an instructor and my grandchildren were students, there would be no partiality. My granddaughters came to school with their dad, but they often stayed with me until I closed the doors at 5:00 each day.

Although my grandchildren call me Nanna, they would have to address me as Dean Chance, just like the other students did, until the end of the school day. My son was also to call me by my title during working hours. Often, as we were leaving school for the day, the girls would ask if I was now Nanna or still Dean Chance. Because of my closeness with all of the students, they also wanted to call me Nanna, but they were told, as my granddaughters had been, at school its Dean Chance. But off campus, at the mall, or other outings I often heard a loud, "Hi Nanna," as the students greeted me.

Another rule I had was with the staff's laptop computers, which had been purchased with funds from the grant. The entire staff was told that the laptops were for classroom preparation only. They were told not to use the computers for personal use as we were under a microscope and needed to do all we could to be in compliance with the Gates Foundation guidelines.

That first year was a great success; the students out-scored the local school district on end of year testing, and even met or exceeded the state scores. There were commendations from local and state boards, as well as the Gates Foundation and the Gates vision was, in fact, working in our small, rural community.

The University President and the Vice President of Academic Affairs, who had originally written the grant and were totally on board with our school, took positions in other universities. After they left, replacements were appointed. Sadly, the new President and VP of Academic Affairs were not buying into our school. They did not visit the students or congratulate them on their successes, and a barrier developed. I could see they didn't really want our school on campus.

At the beginning of the second year, my son was evaluated by the Dean of the School of Education and given a 20 percent raise, along with a new contract for the coming school year. About six weeks into the new term, I received a call to appear at the new President's office. When I arrived, we were joined by the VP of Academic Affairs, the HR Director and the IT Manager. It was explained to me that the IT department had done a sweep on my staffs' laptops and found that one of the instructors had been using a computer for personal use.

My son had broken the rule of no personal use of grant funded computers, it didn't matter how small or what sites were visited. The three most important, powerful people on campus were not willing to allow my son to remain. They refused to take into consideration that he had the highest general math scores in the county with the end of year tests.

When the meeting was over, I walked across campus with a broken heart. I called my son into my office. He was given the option to resign from his position and no issues were placed in his employee file. However, word spread that Dean Chance had fired her son and rumors were numerous about what he had really done. It stuck in my heart that out of his love and devotion for me, he had relocated to a small town that now wasn't even friendly to him.

I tried to immerse myself into my work to ease the sharp edges. The original President and VP had given me a free-hand to make changes and use the foundation's funds in any way I felt was necessary. The new President and VP began questioning my every move. The local superintendent had asked me to meet with him one day and offered me the position of principal of the county's 1,200 student high school.

The prestige and $40,000 increase in salary was a total shock. I really didn't know how to answer. I asked for a few days to think about it, and when we met again, I told him my kids needed me, and I would remain at Early College. So, he also began to withdraw support for our program. Even though my students continued to out-score local and state end of year tests, from here on, there was no mention of their accomplishments.

In the spring of the second year, when my husband again desired to return to work, a local employment agency spoke to him about joining the office as the office manager. There was only one thing left to do—a background check. He reported to work the next day and was rudely told he needed to leave. His criminal history had been reported. Not only did the businessman tell other town businessmen about the guy who might come to them looking for work, but he felt he needed to alert the University President about my husband's criminal history. My husband went home and just about died of depression.

Then it took only a couple of days for me to be called to the University President's office. Of course, we weren't alone, the VP and the HR Director joined us. I was told that living in such a small town my family's indiscretions, first my son's and now my husband's, left them no recourse but to ask for my resignation.

At first I was speechless; I had not seen this coming.

My students were stars. They were doing things in academics no one ever thought they could do; many were enrolled in dual credit college classes, and they were successful. But my words meant nothing to them. I was told they were willing to buy out my contract, and I could use any reason I wanted for my departure.

I believed if I stayed and tried to fight, it would be the program and my students who would lose. I resigned saying, "I have another job offer." I wasn't allowed to explain to my students and staff why I was leaving, but I did meet a few of them off campus later to ask them to stay on track and graduate for me. In fact, 2 years later, I was standing on the sidelines as 44 of the original 50 Gates Foundation students graduated from high school, most of them had 20 or more college credits.

After I left the county, the university and the Bill and Melinda Gates Foundation withdrew their funding. The Early College program was shut down. This good for nothing "elephant" raised his head, roared like a lion, and took the position I had spent years working on and praying for. I had worked hard for my reputation, but it was quickly gone, too.

My husband and I decided we needed to leave this university town and start over elsewhere. When the past Vice President of Academic Affairs had resigned, she had moved to a university in Texas. She told me she would recommend me for a new early college there. I applied and had several phone interviews that I thought were favorable. Soon an offer came. However, all of a sudden, the offer was withdrawn. I hadn't known the extent of the present University President's reach.

We decided we would move to Texas to start over as previously planned. My husband and I put our house on the market and had an offer in two days. We hadn't known that my middle son was being offered a government job in Texas, and he and his family moved outside of Dallas. They offered us the in-law suite in their home.

A yard sale was held where most of our belongings were sold. We took only our most personal items and our cars as we moved west. I again had a heart-breaking decision. I had to leave my oldest son there in this small university town. He had moved home to be near me, now I was leaving him. I knew there was no future for me there, but he decided to stay. Although he was an adult and had his own life to live, wherever he wanted, I felt like he was a small child that I was abandoning. I will forever remember my heart crushing in my chest that day as I drove away.

Chapter 12

"GOD, WHY?"

It was spring when we moved to the new area. We talked about purchasing a retirement home and getting new jobs. We were out and about almost every day, learning and enjoying our new community.

But living with three generations in one house was very difficult. My husband wasn't used to being under someone else's roof and not being in control. I could see his frustrations mounting daily. His frustrations came with outbursts to the grandchildren, which caused my son to speak with him about his words and tone to the kids. I stayed on pins and needles, just praying that there wouldn't be an altercation between my son and my husband. I asked my husband several times for us to move out and get our own apartment. At least until we finalized our plans, but he enjoyed not having to pay monthly living expenses and wouldn't listen to me.

One day in mid-June, my husband had gone out to cut the grass. He decided he didn't want to wear a shirt, just walking shorts. He looked his age and was also packing an extra fifty to sixty pounds. I asked if he would put on the shirt I brought, but he exploded. He couldn't believe I was trying to tell him to do something against his will. How could I believe I knew what was best for him.

He looked filled with rage and told me to get away. It carried on into the evening and through the night; he wouldn't speak to me. I knew he wasn't in bed when I went to sleep, nor was he there the next morning, but I thought he must have come in during the night and had just gotten up early.

When I got up, I found him at the computer, but he still refused to speak to me. I left him alone for about an hour and then I went back into the study to ask him, "What was happening?" Almost word-for-word he said, "I contacted my brother, and he has agreed to let me live with him (back in Alabama). I am taking some files off of the computer that I will need. I am leaving, and I don't want you to say anything to me. This is my decision and I don't need your input."

I just remember saying, "You mean you are going back to visit your brother for awhile." His answer was, "No! I'm going back to stay. You don't love me, and you don't want me here. I'll be gone before lunch." I don't remember anything else.

I kept telling myself to breathe and to stay seated, so I wouldn't fall. The next two hours were a blur, and when he got into his car and drove away, I thought my heart would explode.

For days I spoke very little, just telling the kids that he

had left. I would drive to the mall and sit in the parking lot, crying for hours. I couldn't talk to the kids about what had happened, because I didn't know myself.

Over the next week or so, my husband called twice, but sent several emails. In his messages he was always yelling, the words were all capital letters, two inches high and bolded in red. I didn't know right away that he had stopped at the bank and took most of the money I had saved. I found out from a family member that he was waiting to acquire an Alabama residency, so he could file for a divorce … and … he was going to ask for spousal support.

I had already been left to pay the majority of the bills, and now he wanted me to provide extra money for his living expenses. The money he had taken was basically gone. I saw charges coming on the credit card that I was still responsible for. I knew it would only be a short time before he would max out the accounts. I also knew I would have to make another difficult decision. I had been in Texas long enough to be considered a resident. Now, I would be the one filing for divorce.

For weeks I went from being numb to being tormented with overwhelming mental and emotional pain. I made calls to explain what I thought had happened to extended family members, and after the initial calls, no one mentioned or asked additional questions. It was as though he had never existed. They also knew there was an "elephant" in the corner, and it was best to leave it undisturbed.

Eight months after he left, the trial date was set. I looked for him to be in court that day. I looked for him to want to speak to me—to tell me he had made a mistake and wanted us to stay together—but that didn't happen. The judge granted the divorce. My husband never contacted me again, nor have I seen him since he drove away from the house six years ago.

My husband and I had been married for seventeen years. I knew he had demons, but I thought together we could handle the depression. We always held hands when sitting, standing, or walking together. He had provided physical comfort to me that I had never felt before. The same questions kept going through my thoughts, "God, why? Why did you let this happen to me again? What did I do wrong? Do you even love me?"

The "elephant" was still active, again. "Why God, why can't I find a man to love, to hold and care for me? Why am I the bad seed?" There appeared to be no light in my life, only darkness.

Those days, weeks, and months from June to October were an emotional storm. I started looking for jobs to free myself from the constant minute-by-minute replay of what had happened. I received an offer to move to Waco, Texas, to teach in a middle school for at-risk students. I felt to start over, I had to put aside my advanced degree and return to the classroom, where I had done my best work.

I was living about 100 miles away from my son and his family. I had to start over in many ways, no furniture, little money, no family or friends close by, and no self-worth. For the very first time in my entire life, I was living alone, there was no one to greet me when I came home, or ask me how I felt, or wish me a good night. I seldom left the house, except to go to work.

In the midst of this lonely time, the word came that my half-brother, from my father, had suddenly died. It had been three years since I had seen my brothers and sister at Mother's funeral, and I wasn't sure what reactions there would be when I attended the funeral.

My son was out of town, so my daughter-in-law and the three grandchildren took the six-hour drive with me to my brother's service. We arrived the night before. The next morning when we arrived at the funeral home, my brother and sister had already arrived. Since for the past seven years they had refused to speak with me, I didn't want to cause a disruption. So when I entered the lobby and saw them, I went to the other side and took a seat. It seemed like hours before we were invited to gather in the family room for a final prayer before going into the chapel. We stood a few minutes as the pastor spoke of my brother's life.

While standing there on the other side of the room, I felt alone—like on a desert island. I believed there would never be any more contact with my family. But when I finally lifted my eyes, I made eye contact with my sister. We both said, "I love you." In seconds we were sobbing in each others' arms. My brother patted me on the back, but gave no hug. We walked out of the chapel, telling each other how much we had missed the other, and how much we wanted to build a relationship we never really had. She was unable to go to the cemetery and needed to leave right away, so we parted, but promised to get together soon.

When I got back in the car after the grave-side service, my sister had left a voice message saying, "I may have lost my brother today, but I got my sister back." I returned her call immediately. I wanted to know when I could see her again, but making those plans would not be easy.

The school year was closing in Waco, so I made the decision to resign my teaching position, and move back home to Alabama. I felt I had to rebuild the relationship with my siblings that had been broken way too long. My sister and I spoke on the phone several times, but couldn't find the time to meet. She didn't live back home, but would only be about four hours away.

For the first month after I moved back home, I rented a house and prepared myself to go back to teaching. This time, it was in the same school my three sons and their father had attended. I had been away from the area for a long time, and it was almost like moving to a new town. I was consumed with getting resettled and making plans for the challenges the new school year would bring. My sister and I kept talking and making plans to meet soon, but time got away from us.

As I prepared to leave the rental house the first day of school, I received a phone call, my sister had died overnight from a brain aneurysm. I didn't know the few minutes at my brother's funeral would be the last time I would see her. In emergency surgery, they had shaved her head and no one except her husband and children would be allowed to see her after she died.

Again, I asked God a question, "God, why would you bring her back into my life to take her away too soon?" She was gone, and so were my dreams of rebuilding the family I had lost. My brother-in-law had not accepted our plans to meet and decided to leave me out of most of the family activities. Even during the service, I was not allowed to sit with the immediate family.

Those three days were a blur. There was a visitation, a family meal, and a service, but I couldn't feel anything. I stood when they said stand and sat at other times. My three sons and their families had come from Texas, Louisiana, and Georgia, to be with me. They gave me as much support as possible. The day after the funeral they decided they needed to return to their homes, and I decided I should go back to work, rather than just sit at home alone and grieve for my sister.

What I had seen as the building of a relationship

with my sister ended. I knew my sister was gone, but just maybe I could rebuild a relationship with my brother. He and I had grown up with only ourselves as playmates. We seldom had neighbors near Mother's house; we just had each other. Perhaps what had occurred over the past three months was too much, too fast. I would need to give him room to invite me in.

The day I returned to work I was trying to move past the extreme emptiness I felt. That afternoon when I returned to the rental house, the day after burying my sister, I found someone had broken the door and stolen the new, just purchased, large screen TV. I had little funds to purchase new items, but was doing the best I could. I yelled, "God, where were You? Why do You let these things keep happening to me? Don't You care? Why God? Why? I know You say You will only put on us what is in our ability to carry, but God, I can't carry this burden. Help me, God!"

I stayed at the rental house another week until the new house I was purchasing was ready. This was an unusual feeling. I was moving into a house I alone had chosen, with furniture that I alone had selected. I had to rebuild my life, yet again. Our small town was home to several extended family members, as well as my only remaining sibling. I was able to purchase a beautiful new home. It was my show case with a large in ground pool, a beautiful garden, and a designated bird sanctuary, all of which was an ideal place for parties.

Over the months, the family attended several parties,

but I wasn't invited to theirs. I had been away from home almost twenty years and they had their own circle of family and friends, which didn't include me in their activities. I tried to include my brother in my life, but he chose to limit his involvement with me.

Three months later, I drove about sixty miles to visit my oldest son and his family for Thanksgiving. I returned home on Black Friday to find that there had been another break-in. My new house had been vandalized. The side door had been kicked in, and the brand new, large screen TV and family jewelry were gone. This jewelry could never be replaced. The house was in disarray. My belongings had been pulled from the drawers and closets and thrown around the rooms.

After the police had come and gone, no family came to see about me. I noticed the thieves had closed all the blinds in the house. I wondered what they had done while in my home. I didn't even want to touch my belongings. I sat alone in the living room, just looking out on the manicured lawn. The birds were taking their final flights before heading south for the winter, the beauty outside hid the ugliness on the inside—much the way I felt about my own self. It was another financial burden, but the emotional one was far greater. "What is so wrong with me? Why? Why me? Why now? Will this ever end!? How much more do I have to endure?"

For months I taught school, but spent many hours

alone. My brother had been courteous but cold. He didn't seem to want to mend our broken relationship. I thought I had accomplished the career high, me a dean. I thought I had the man of my dreams, who had vowed "till death us do part," but he was now also gone. I continued to look for peace of heart, but I couldn't find it. I had overestimated my own accomplishments. It was God Who deserved the glory.

I prayed again, "God, why am I alone? Why am I deserted? I am at the end of my road, and I don't know where to go." I felt abandoned by God and everyone around me. I became bitter, blaming God for the hardships I was facing. Answers still didn't come. The "elephant" in the corner had become so huge it was taking over my life. "Where do I go? What do I become?" I'm a failure in the eyes of my family, friends, and all who know me. "God, where is my peace? What value is there to my life? God what could I possibly do that would benefit others?"

After months of praying, God put a different prayer in my heart. Going home had been my peace, not His. I can't say the decision was easy, but I put my house on the market to sell, which was a huge loss. I resigned from the teaching position.

In the summer of 2011, I took several road trips to try and find that place where I could belong. I visited a retirement community in Florida, but there was no warmth there. I visited my son in Georgia, but knew the university town couldn't bring me joy. I visited my youngest son in Louisiana, but felt no connection with the community. I worked my way back to the Dallas/Fort Worth area.

I sent several resumes to school districts, thinking that education must be my purpose. I accepted a position as a consultant for a private school near Dallas. But ninety days later, I realized I had made the decision on my own without His direction. I thought I had to be working in my career field, but I realized I wasn't allowing God to have control over my life. So, I resigned the new position and began my peace-seeking journey.

Chapter 13

GATEWAY TO PEACE

Now, for the rest of the story. Although my son and his family lived in Keller, Texas, since 2008, and visited several churches, they had not yet given their membership to a church. One weekend, we visited a church called Gateway in Southlake, Texas. The message was delivered by the church Pastor, Robert Morris, but it didn't take a second visit for me to know I had finally come home. I had been a member of several churches, but all of them had less than a hundred attendees. Gateway, at that time, had 24,000 members. Could I find a place in such a large church?

When I think about my family and how I felt like I was emotionally neglected, I am sure they didn't see it that way. I am sure my mother was doing the best she could. When I didn't hear the words, "I love you," it wasn't because she didn't. Since her death I have discovered that her family seldom used those words to express their feelings. I know that words can't always bring comfort, but what comes from the heart does.

In my teens during a revival, I felt God calling me to be

a missionary. But I couldn't imagine going to a remote part of the world, fighting bugs, living in a grass hut and wondering if my neighbors would eat me for breakfast.

When God told Jonah to, "Go," he went in the opposite direction. That's exactly what I did. Because of Jonah's refusal to follow God's directions, he spent three days and nights in the belly of a whale. However, I wish my situation had only taken this long. For me, wandering in my own desert took more than the forty years it took the Israelites to find their Promised Land. I had been called to work with throw-away children, but I was following my own directions.

I don't even believe my husband had any choice in the decisions he made; I believe God needed to get my attention. I had lived my life thinking I could only find peace with a man's physical comfort and a grand career. I may even have seen my angel as an independent agent.

Fifty years ago, when I could have died, I should have carved those words, "You can't come now, you have to go back," into my heart, knowing that God had a bigger and better plan for me than I could ever know. I prayed for God to give me the courage to dream dreams, the faithfulness to wait for His timing, and to give me the strength that only He could provide.

I had run from my calling to serve others for so long. I thought God had given up on me, but He hadn't. I felt I had been a good person, attended church from time to time, and had given money to the church when I had extra to give. What else did I have to do?

In despair, I went to my knees in prayer, not once, but several times daily. I began reading the Bible again, but now I had eyes to see and ears to hear. I was beginning to understand the verses I had read so many times before. God was speaking to me through His words. I remember praying, "God I don't know where or when I got off course, but I know I have not become the daughter you created me to be. I am asking that you use me. Give me a service to do for others."

There are many times in our lives that we believe we are not good enough to fill a purpose from God. If you doubt your value to God, read the second chapter of Joshua. The Israelites were ready to enter the Promised Land. The two spies Joshua sent to scout out Jericho came to the house of Rahab—a prostitute. Why would God use someone with such a sinful past? God will often use people with simple faith to accomplish His great purposes. It is only our lack of faith that makes us believe He will choose only the most righteous to fill a need. No matter how insignificant we may feel, God can use us where we are in ways that are far greater than we can imagine.

During the years of abuse, I had hoped to be rescued by my knight in shining armor, but my angel came in silence instead. I was thirty-five years old when my father passed away. I wasted all those years waiting for an apology from him, an apology that never came. I now know that what really needed to happen—first—was for me to forgive myself. I had blamed myself for not being good enough, the bad seed. But I know I have a Father in Heaven Who loves me. I was made in His image and I am not a bad seed. I have since learned to forgive my earthly father and find peace for those troubling years.

When I was married twice to the father of my children, I assumed I was the cause for his adultery. I felt I wasn't woman enough to keep him at home with me and our children. My hopes were always that the boys could develop a relationship with their father, because I never wanted to fill the role of both parents. I kept hoping they would build some good times. When he died about twelve years ago of cancer, they each had developed their own special relationship with him.

When I was held against my will, I know the angel spoke to the man for me. It was as if I was Moses and didn't have the words, but God provided the angel to speak through me. During many difficult years, I chose to think of myself only in the way others saw me. I believed I deserved the abuse and there was no way out. I was too weak to handle the situation alone.

Those nights when I thought my ex-husband would kill me, I was resigned to die. I remember him sensing my angel in the room, although he didn't acknowledge her. I knew she was there protecting me and that I would survive. Those times and situations when my angel stepped in and brought me through the valleys of possible death, why didn't I listen to God Who was there all the time? Instead, I kept digging my own valley.

Over the days and weeks of constantly being in prayer and the Word, I felt God's hand bringing me peace. I found my calling at Gateway Church, serving others through Food Services. At first I would volunteer to serve on the weekends, and then it spread to Monday night Single Parent Meals, and to the Prayer Shawl Ministry.

Today, just over two years at Gateway Church, I work part-time in foodservice as a crew lead and can proudly say I am home. I have a Father Who loves me, Who has forgiven all my sins, and a family who loves and accepts me just as I am. I have found my service to do, each week as I serve pastors, leaders, members and guests. I believe God allowed me to stumble for so long, all the while waiting for me to return.

I know He wasn't the One Who left—I was. He was right where I left Him. He is the same yesterday, today and tomorrow.

A poem was written years ago about someone who was going through a hard, difficult time. They were walking in the sand. When they only saw one set of footprints, they began to question God about why they were left alone during their struggles. It's then that the Lord revealed that the footsteps were His ... He was actually carrying the person. Just like this poem, when you don't think you can go any further, God carries you.

When I was born a preemie, I can only sense the directions God must have given my angel, "She may look small right now, but I have big things for her. She will stray from the course I have planned, but protect her in her travels through life, until she returns to me."

Chapter 14

"NEVER, NEVER GIVE UP"

You and I were created in the image of God. He knew us before we were ever born. From the time of Adam and Eve, there have been choices to make in our lives. God told Adam not to eat from of the tree of knowledge of good and evil, but Adam didn't listen, he made a different choice and our lives were forever changed.

As with Adam and Eve, you and I were created with the ability to freely choose for ourselves the directions we would also take. Many times those choices are contrary to the will of God, but He gives us the freedom to choose. He never demands that we follow His will. If He did, we would all be robots, not humans.

But God is patient with us, pursuing us in love with a desire to salvage a loving relationship. Think about the story of Balaam in the Book of Numbers. God had given him directions to follow, but Balaam sought worldly gain. It was his donkey who was able to see the Angel of the Lord that was blocking his way. Balaam was blinded by his own greed and was saved by a simple donkey. What person or thing will cause you to finally be able to see God's direction?

If you find yourself in an abusive situation, always know there is a way out. Take a moment to read John 8:1-12. The story is about a woman who was caught in the act of adultery. When the town's people found out what she had done, they wanted to punish her by stoning her to death, which was the custom at that time.

The men from the town dragged the woman to where Jesus was teaching. The Pharisees and other teachers of the law wanted Jesus to pass judgment on the woman. Instead, Jesus bent over and started writing on the ground, not answering their question. When they asked again, He rose and said, "If any of you is without sin, let him be the first to throw a stone at her." Then, Jesus bent down and wrote on the ground again.

Stop ... and listen! Do you hear the rocks falling to the ground? The men of the village dropped the rocks as they walked away. They no longer were going to throw the rocks at the woman, but now the stones were being tossed aside. They knew they were not without sin.

In that scene, I can see the woman lying on the ground battered, bleeding, and sobbing. Jesus stood again and spoke to the woman saying, "Woman, where are your accusers? Has no one condemned you?" She answered, "No one, sir." Then Jesus told her, "Then neither do I condemn you. Go now and leave your life of sin." Jesus had taken the woman's sins onto Himself.

What God has planned for me is far greater than what anybody else believed of me. When Jesus went to the cross, His burdens were heavy. He was taking all of our sins. When you pray and ask God to take control of the situation, He will. Our Heavenly Father will take action on every prayer that comes out of a heart of faith. That doesn't mean the outcome will always be just what you wanted. God may give you a detour to get you back on the course He had planned, but you must let go first.

Do you remember what it was like when you were learning to ride a bike? As long as your parent or someone else was holding on to the bike, you weren't on your own. Your parent had to let go. God knows far better than we do how long to hold on and when to let go. He knows exactly what it will take to fix your mess. However, it's difficult for God to lead you, if you want to hold on to certain parts—if you want to do things your own way. You've got to learn to let go! He's got you!

None of us have all the answers, but God does. How often do you ask for His blessings? When no one believes in you, believe in yourself. Our road to spiritual maturity takes many turns and is an ongoing challenge that is never-ending. Every road creates challenges and opportunities. We should seek God's guidance in each road we take. Walk in faith and never lose hope.

How complete is your faith? When Elijah asked the

widow for food, how strong was her faith? She told him she had only enough to make a last meal for herself and her son. Elijah told her that everything would be fine, in fact, if she used the last flour and oil she had to make bread for him, her flour and oil would not run out before the Lord sent rain.

Take a moment and put yourself in her kitchen. Do you think she waited for a "poof" to magically fill her bin first before she baked the bread for Elijah? The Word tells us she gave Elijah the bread first, and then the miracle occurred. Don't wait for a miracle before you share your faith. God is trying to lead you along the path of His choosing, but he won't force you to follow. God has given you free will, and the choices are yours.

What if you awoke today and the only things left were what you had prayed for yesterday, what would you still have? Would you have lost your family, health, or wealth because you didn't pray for them? Would you have prayed for your church or your nation? Would you have been too busy to be bothered to pray? Would your prayer have been rote and nothing specific came to mind? Or would the things dearest to you, like your family, church, health, resources, and nation have been in your prayers yesterday and are still strong today?

How often do you pray—just before going to sleep at night or right after you wake up? God, the Father, Jesus, His Son, the Holy Spirit and I have a party line. I don't wait until I am stuck in traffic and say, "By the way Lord, I'm stuck in traffic. Can you move these cars so I can get home?" My call is never disconnected. I don't have to wait for dial-up. I just say, "Hello Father," and the prayers flow, never ceasing.

I continue to read the Bible and be in prayer throughout each day. My brain seems to be stretched across the cosmos with the new, profound knowledge that I am gaining.

I can now see clearer when I hear the message, music, and friends, as they speak of their own relationships with Him. I can finally say, "Yes, I know Him." I have so much more to learn—so much more to experience. I keep making adjustments in my life to walk completely by faith. God is tweaking my life day-by-day. God hasn't called everyone to do what I do. God had plans for me that He may not have for others. However, He still has a plan for you!

Being attentive to God works out our priorities or the things we count as being important. If you haven't discovered your passionate pursuit that blesses you and others, don't become discouraged … keep searching and believing that God will show you how to serve yourself, others, and Him. Don't walk your path alone. God builds us through challenges we face.

Being a Christian means you must be alert each day as you go about your activities to fulfill what God has in store for you. Only God knows how your life can impact others. He may not give you a huge assignment, but you can expect He has an assignment only you can fill. When you are faithful in the small things, maybe ordinary tasks, there is no telling what the extent of your next task will be.

When God is pleased with where you are, then He will promote you. Being in the center of God's will or direction can break your heart. Sometimes, we just don't understand God's timing in our lives with death and other struggles, but remember, God has an army of angels to light your way. If you think you have just passed through or are in the midst of the storm, look for the rainbow.

My message to you as you read my story is, "Never, Never Give Up," but allow God to lead. He had your path planned and developed before you were ever born. What is success to the world may not be in God's timing. You're not finished until God says you're finished.

As Christ did at the Mount of Olives, we, too, must face trials that bring fear and the unknown. We sometimes hurt to the very depths of our soul, but when we are willing to accept God's will, we can experience the peace that only He can bring. When you reach a fork in your road, let God lead you; He knows the path. God wants us to follow His will obediently. He has predetermined ways He would like for us to respond to, but we have the choice to do them or not.

I know I have so much more to learn, experience, and share. I can't wait for each new day. Will you surrender your struggles today? What do you have to lose? Instead, you have so much to gain. Sharing what God is doing in your life can help others. Every one of God's children has a story to tell. What is yours?

God's plan is for us to accept our past struggles, take to heart the present, and trust His hands in our future. Two years ago when I began this fantastic journey, I prayed, "God please hear me one more time." But God doesn't keep count of how many times we start over. He doesn't count the "one more time." There will never be an end to His forgiveness.

Today and always my prayer is, "Lord, let my actions and deeds serve as my testimony to the miracles you have performed in my life. Give me the courage to meet every struggle, the strength to overcome any trial, and the wisdom to accept your peace. God, here am I. Send me."

I leave you with the Special Olympic motto, "Let me win, but if I cannot win, let me be brave in the attempt."

www.ingramcontent.com/pod-product-compliance
Lightning Source LLC
Chambersburg PA
CBHW071007040426
42443CB00007B/696